Trading Beyond the Patterns

OrangeBooks Publication

1st Floor, Rajhans Arcade, Mall Road, Kohka, Bhilai, Chhattisgarh 490020

Website: **www.orangebooks.in**

© Copyright, 2024, Author

All rights reserved. No part of this book may be reproduced, stored in a retrieval system, or transmitted, in any form by any means, electronic, mechanical, magnetic, optical, chemical, manual, photocopying, recording or otherwise, without the prior written consent of its writer.

First Edition, 2024
ISBN: 978-93-5621-516-0

TRADING BEYOND THE PATTERNS

The Psychology of Winning in Markets

ABHAY PATIL

OrangeBooks Publication
www.orangebooks.in

An Introductory From The Author

Growing up in a small town in India, I was a curious and ambitious boy, always dreaming about my future and how I could become the pillar of support for my family. My goal was clear: to learn, achieve something extraordinary, and make my loved ones proud. While many dream, only a few make it happen, and that's exactly what I want to share with you.

In India, we often hear about staying safe in our careers and lives, following a path that promises security. But I saw something different. Even though my family was relatively comfortable, the idea of settling into a routine and growing within the same safe space didn't sit well with me. I noticed the stagnant growth around me and knew I wanted more than just security. I craved the freedom to explore beyond the usual and achieve financial independence.

My journey towards financial freedom began at the age of 15. I remember sitting on the last bench in school with my friends, daydreaming about business ideas and imagining ourselves making huge profits someday. As days passed, my determination to do something significant only grew stronger. After finishing my 10th board exams, while others saw the vacation as a time to relax, I saw it as an opportunity. I started small, making modest profits, but I constantly pushed myself out of my comfort zone, seeking more significant challenges and rewards. This drive not only strengthened me financially but also built my mental resilience.

Every experience taught me something new and pushed me to aim higher. I realized that the key to breaking free from the average 'middle-class mindset' was to strive for more than just getting by. Despite coming from a reasonably well-off family, we faced financial ups and downs that affected us deeply. These moments of financial strain and instability made me even more determined to avoid the trap of settling for less and to be the guiding light for my family.

Years ago, I knew that relying solely on the market wasn't enough; developing a powerful psychological mindset was crucial. My journey through trading and the markets wasn't just about the numbers but about mastering the psychology behind them. I achieved significant success because I understood the patterns of winning markets, and I want to share this wisdom with you.

In this book, "Trading Beyond the Patterns: The Psychology of Winning in Markets," I aim to guide you through understanding and mastering the psychological aspects of trading. It's not just about strategies and predictions; it's about cultivating a mindset that allows you to thrive in the world of trading

Abstract

Everyone has many goals in life, but only some people achieve them. Your brain is the key player in this game, and your heart tries to follow its lead. In this book, I will show you the great power of your mind and how it can make your dreams come true. REMEMBER: Everyone dreams, but few make it happen. My aim is to help you become one of those who do. Always remember, it's mostly your mind and a bit of your skills. This is YOU vs. YOU.

Whenever you look for solutions to your problems, they are already in your mind. But to find them, you need to keep your brain active. This book will show you how to do that. Learn to see what holds you back. What are your fears? What limits you? For many, it's self-doubt and a negative mindset. Keep your head up and keep moving forward.

Do you often think, 'What if this doesn't work for me?' But have you tried it first? We need to break these doubts and myths. They can hold you back easily, affecting your willpower and making you think negatively about yourself. Every day, you see yourself in the mirror, and if these doubts win, your enthusiasm will quickly disappear. Imagine losing all your progress and starting from zero. If someone asks you, 'What stopped you?' Do you want to answer, 'Self-doubt?' Of course not! Instead, imagine someone asking, 'How did you achieve so much? Please help me do the same...' Sounds better, right? This shows the power you have to influence others. Understanding these psychological patterns can help you succeed.

I truly believe you can do this, and I'm here to support you on your journey to success. I will help you solve the problems that hold you back and teach you how to master your mind. On this journey, we won't limit ourselves mentally. We will build an empire you are capable of ruling. Let's grow and learn together without limits. Get ready... especially mentally

Limits of Applicability

The author and publisher have taken great care in preparing this material. However, they make no guarantees about the content, recognizing that interpretations can vary among readers. They will not be responsible for any losses or damages, including special, incidental, or consequential damages, that may result from the use of this book.

This publication is meant for general informational purposes and is not a replacement for professional advice. It may not be suitable for every individual and does not offer personalized recommendations.

Contents

An Introductory From The Author v
Abstract viii
Limits of Applicability xi

Section - 1
Constant Drive for Success in Trading 1

1.1 A Wake-Up Call for Financial Freedom okay 1
1.2 The Treasure of Knowledge and Mastery 3
1.3 The Adrenaline Rush Through Markets.. 8
1.4 Striving for Personal Accomplishments and Goals 12
1.5 The Setbacks of Not Succeeding 15
1.6 The Social and Community Building 19

Section - 2
Directing the Mental Strata of Emotions 23

2.1 The Illusion of Get Rich Quick: Exposing the Myth of Easy Money 23
2.2 Merging Emotions: Fright to Greed Displayed 26
2.3 How Overconfidence Consumes You And Your Success...................................30

2.4 Guide You Through An Unstructured Roadmap Takes You To Failure 37
2.5 Building a Seasoned Mindset Before Becoming a Trader: Overcoming Analysis Paralysis and Cultivating Psychological Resilience 47
2.6 The Cons of Falling for Trading Myths: A Way Out for Indian Traders 53

Section - 3
Planting A Winning Mindset 61

3.1 Path to Consistent Success 61
3.2 The Ultimate Power of Visualization.....68
3.3 Setting Yourself Up for the Long-Term.75

Section - 4
Begin To Not Put An End 81

4.1 Traders' Initial Journey and Breakthrough 81
4.2 Expectations, Mentorship, and All About Starting Out 86
4.3 The Ultimate Call............................94

Section - 1
Constant Drive for Success in Trading

1.1 A Wake-Up Call for Financial Freedom okay

In a country like India, where every struggling citizen dreams of financial independence, many of you reading this might resonate deeply with the journey ahead. It's never too late to turn your life around, no matter the hurdles and struggles you face. Most of us yearn to break free from the traditional mindset of working tirelessly in a job that brings its own set of challenges and constraints.

Every day, you might see friends or acquaintances earning three times more than you but still unable to find time for family, friends, or even themselves. They hesitate to ask for a simple break to breathe. The stark reality is that, despite the difference in income, both of you are trapped in the same unending cycle of what we call 'professional' labor. This constant grind drains your emotions, making it hard to think practically and rationally.

It's disheartening how many of us continually strive and work excessively just to grasp a fleeting sense of freedom—freedom to live life on our own terms. Having spent over a decade in trading, I can confidently tell you that in the world of trading, you are your own boss and your own employee. The only person you compete with daily is yourself, and your true enemies are the impulsive decisions that can trap you in the same cage the world has built for you

Trading offers you the chance to explore numerous opportunities to achieve your dreams. Imagine waking up each day with the knowledge that you have the power to shape your financial destiny. No longer will you be tied down by the exhausting routine of a 9-to-5 job, struggling to please others just to earn a bit more than average.

This is a call to all those waiting for a sign—this might be it! Trading is not just about the markets; it's about taking control of your life. In the next chapter, I will show you how you can build the lifestyle you've always dreamed of. It's time to take the first step towards your financial freedom and transform your life in ways you once only imagined.

1.2 The Treasure of Knowledge and Mastery

Just like the radiant tapestry of India's cultural landscape, there lies a deeply-rooted tradition of treasuring and esteeming education and knowledge. We hold pride in our teaching and learning and so as to keep a similar positive mindset about achieving your goal we forget to do the same. Formation of ancient centers of education such as Nalanda and Takshashila to the modern-day institutions of academic brilliance, the utmost treasuring of knowledge has been a key feature of Indian society. The adoration for learning goes beyond the confines of conventional academia. This surpasses each and every aspect of our lives and similarly plays a role in the dynamic world of trading.

Trading, with knowledge of technical analysis, strategy, planning and decision-making appeals naturally to those with an intention and hunger for intellectual spark. In the realm of trading where the mind is constantly challenged and worked where every trade gives you a chance to learn and grow. Many individuals like you, who are eager and willing to thrive continuously expand their understanding of the markets, trading resources a playground for them of unending winning possibilities. Despite the affection of trading and the abundance of handful resources available to expanding traders, many in our country remain hesitant to venture into this exponentially growing domain. The reasons cannot be measured on fingers, but the king among those reasons is the influence of the traditional Indian mindset, which often views trading with skepticism and is considered as an unconventional practice. A mindset that is rooted to common perspective is a caution and in assumption to established norms, and to delve in fear of the unknown.

But what if I told you that trading which is wrapped around with the assumptions and practices of so called 'gamble' they call it, is a disciplined practice and routine grounded in knowledge to master this skill? What if I prove to you that by encouraging the principles of trading, you can unlock a roadmap to financial freedom and self-fulfillment? And the answer to all this question is the power that your brain holds for you to excel. Trading is not simply about buying and selling assets; it is about understanding the market behavior which is indirectly studying human behavior. Learning market dynamics and taking strategic steps is not preventable. It is purely a skill that rewards those who are willing to put in the effort to educate themselves and develop their analytical abilities, and to cultivate the punctuality and patience that is necessary to navigate you to manage the rough seas of the market.

The markets help you study much like life itself. It is complex and constantly ever-changing. They resist prediction, build conventional wisdom within the markets, and challenge the very notion of certainty that means as a seasoned trader you would just know how the market will be reacting. With all this chaos lies a hidden order, a pattern, a picture waiting to be disclosed by the accurate observer. It is this ability of understanding the ultimatum of mindset mastery, that sets the successful trader apart from the rest struggling to survive. Although knowledge alone is not enough, mastering a skill requires the 4 P's- Practice, Patience, Perseverance, and Punctuality and a directive mindset of course.

In this journey you should be willing to appreciate failure as a journey step to success. Don't see setbacks as obstacles but instead take advantage of it to find opportunities to grow. One needs thorough humility to study markets which are indifferent to those with pride and not guaranteed to the weak ones. In the journey towards mastery, there will be moments of self-doubt, moments of frustration, moments when the temptation becomes almost irresistible and you might lose it all. A true trader reveals themselves, accumulating the courage to stay the course, to trust in their abilities, and to hold the ropes tight during adverse situations. So, to all those who yearn for financial independence, to all those who want to break free from the cage of conventional wisdom, I recommend: Treasure knowledge and mastery won't be any far. Practice trading not as a gamble, but as a disciplined craft that rewards dedication and diligence. And above all, plant a mindset of unwavering belief to discover that potential in you.

For in the world of trading, as in life, the only limits are those we place upon ourselves. So, take off the chains you hold of doubts, seek your destiny, and embark upon a journey of discovery that will lead you to levels beyond your wildest imagination. The path to mastery awaits; are you ready to take the first step?

1.3 The Adrenaline Rush Through Markets

For many, trading isn't just about amassing wealth—it's about the exhilarating rush that comes with every market move. The thrill of executing a well-timed trade, watching your predictions unfold, and seeing your capital grow is akin to the passion and enthusiasm we find in cricket or Bollywood. It's about savoring the highs and lows and cherishing the journey.

Picture this: You're at your desk, eyes locked on the bright screen displaying the market's ups and downs, fingers poised over the keyboard. The market pulses with life, every candlestick a new opportunity. As you analyze and execute a perfectly timed trade, there it is—the surge of adrenaline that keeps traders coming back for more, pushing their limits. This is where you learn to navigate and understand the intricate dance of the market.

Trading offers a unique experience, a rollercoaster of emotions that rivals the excitement of any sport or movie. Just as cricket fans leap with joy at a boundary or Bollywood enthusiasts are swept away by a gripping scene, traders are immersed in the drama of the markets. In a world where fortunes can be made or lost in an instant, every minute brings the potential for victory or defeat. What makes trading so thrilling? Part of it is the inherent unpredictability of the markets. Unlike a scripted film, the markets operate on their own terms, defying logic and reason. This unpredictability amplifies the adrenaline rush, making each trade a high-stakes venture with the promise of untold rewards.

But it's not just the thrill of the chase that captivates traders—it's also the sense of mastery and control that comes from successfully navigating the markets. You become someone others look to for guidance, your expertise making you a trusted figure. Just as a skilled cricketer thrives on the challenge of facing a fast bowler or an actor embraces the complexity of a demanding role, traders revel in the intellectual challenge of analyzing trends and making split-second decisions.

Trading is also an art. Like an artist studying their subject before sketching, traders delve into charts, market movements, and consumer behaviors to make informed decisions. This process is a delicate balance between artistry and analysis, risk and reward. It's about interpreting the subtle cues in the data and uncovering patterns that reveal the market's true intentions. When everything aligns, when your predictions prove accurate and your strategy succeeds, the rush is incomparable—a triumph that validates your skills and fuels your passion.

Of course, with the highs of trading come the inevitable lows. Just as a cricketer must learn to accept defeat or an actor must withstand harsh reviews, traders must cope with the market's ups and downs. This is a lesson in resilience, in bouncing back from setbacks with even greater determination.

One of the most rewarding aspects of trading is the camaraderie and community among traders. Much like the bonds formed among cricket teammates or film cast members, traders build strong connections through their shared passion for the markets. Whether exchanging tips on online forums or meeting at conferences, traders find support and encouragement in each other's company.

In the end, trading is about more than just making money—it's about the thrill of the chase, the surge of adrenaline, and the bonds forged with fellow traders. It's about embracing life in all its fast-paced, vibrant intensity, welcoming the highs and lows alike, and appreciating the journey with all its twists and turns. So, gear up, fellow traders, and prepare for the ride of a lifetime—the market awaits, and the adrenaline rush is calling your name.

1.4 Striving for Personal Accomplishments and Goals

Trading is more than just numbers on a screen or the fluctuations of the market. It's a powerful tool that can help you achieve personal accomplishments and goals that might seem out of reach through traditional means. While in a conventional job you often follow instructions, in trading, you leverage your intellect and persistence to chart your own path to success. Becoming a successful trader turns you into a visual thinker, someone who believes in incremental progress—each calculated move bringing you closer to your dreams.

Imagine this: you've always wanted to provide the best education for your children, to see them soar and reach their fullest potential. In today's world, where education can cost a fortune, this dream often feels like a distant hope. This is where trading steps in. With its potential for significant returns, trading can provide the funds necessary to secure your children's future, ensuring they have access to the opportunities and resources they need to succeed.

But securing a bright future for your loved ones is just one aspect. Trading can fuel countless personal goals and aspirations. Perhaps you've always dreamed of owning your own home, a stable and secure haven where you can build your life and create priceless memories. Or maybe you've longed to travel the world, exploring new cultures and experiencing the richness of diverse destinations. Whatever your dreams, trading offers the potential to turn them into reality.

Take Ravi's story, for instance. Ravi, a software engineer from Bangalore, always dreamed of owning a home in his bustling city. For over a decade, he worked tirelessly, saving every penny in the hopes of one day achieving his dream. But it wasn't until he discovered the world of trading that he realized the true potential of his savings. With careful analysis and strategic investing, Ravi grew his wealth exponentially, enabling him to finally purchase his dream home and secure a brighter future for his family.

Or consider Priya, an entrepreneur from Mumbai with a passion for travel. For years, Priya dreamed of embarking on a once-in-a-lifetime trip around the world. Yet, the demands of running her own business made this dream seem perpetually out of reach. That was until she discovered the power of trading. By dedicating herself to learning the intricacies of the market and taking calculated risks, Priya was able to fund her dream trip and experience the adventure of a lifetime.

These are just two of the many inspiring stories of Indian traders who have used their success in trading to achieve significant personal milestones and become pillars of support for those around them. Their journeys remind us that trading can transform lives and help us achieve our fullest potential.

Whether it's funding your child's education, buying your dream home, or embarking on that long-desired adventure, trading can turn even the most ambitious dreams into reality. To those who dare to dream and refuse to let fear or doubt hold them back, I say: embrace the power of trading. Watch as each day of progress brings your dreams to life. The journey may be challenging, the path may be rugged, but with dedication, determination, and belief in your potential, you can achieve your goals. Dream big, and let trading be the key that unlocks a future filled with endless possibilities.

1.5 The Setbacks of Not Succeeding

In the exhilarating world of trading, the potential rewards are immense. However, it's essential to acknowledge the significant risks that come with every trade. While success can lead to financial freedom and personal fulfillment, failure can take a heavy toll, both financially and emotionally, often leaving one demotivated and shaken. In this chapter, we delve into the harsh realities of trading failures and emphasize the importance of psychological readiness, preparedness, and discipline to manage and mitigate these risks effectively.

Trading isn't for the faint-hearted or those who give up at the first sign of trouble. It demands courage, resilience, and a willingness to embrace uncertainty with every decision. Despite meticulous planning and comprehensive market analysis, there are no guarantees in trading. Prices can flip unexpectedly, trends can reverse without warning, and even the most experienced traders can find themselves on the losing side of a trade.

The consequences of trading failures can be profound, impacting both your finances and emotional well-being. The allure of quick wealth often blinds many to the inherent risks of trading, leading to impulsive decisions and rash behavior. In an instant, fortunes can disappear, dreams can be dashed, and lives can be upended, leaving traders to start over from scratch, but now burdened with fear and caution.

Consider the story of Rajesh, a young trader from Delhi. Tempted by the promise of easy money in the stock market through enticing schemes like "Double your wealth," Rajesh jumped into trading with minimal understanding of its principles, driven by greed and the desire for quick profits. He made increasingly risky bets, blinded by the prospect of rapid gains. But when the market turned against him, Rajesh found himself overwhelmed by debt, his savings depleted, and his confidence shattered. This story of Rajesh is a stark reminder of the dangers of unreliable guidance and the consequences of underestimating the complexities of trading.

Rajesh's experience underscores the harsh realities of trading and the vital importance of humility and caution in the face of uncertainty. However, it also highlights the resilience of the human spirit. Despite his setbacks, Rajesh refused to let his failures define him. He chose to learn from his mistakes, adapt, and grow as a trader, ultimately finding success on his own terms.

Navigating the turbulent waters of the market requires more than just technical know-how or financial acumen. It demands psychological preparedness and emotional resilience. It's about maintaining the discipline to resist temptations, staying true to your trading plan even when faced with uncertainty. Recognizing that failure isn't the end, but rather the beginning of a new learning journey, is crucial.

To all those who dare to venture into trading, I offer this advice: approach the markets with confidence but never ignore the risks. Commit to continuous self-improvement. Learn from the mistakes of others, but also be ready to make your own and grow from them. Trading is a path filled with challenges and setbacks, but with the right mindset and perseverance, it can lead to extraordinary accomplishments.

1.6 The Social and Community Building

In Indian culture, community and social support form the ropes that bind individuals together in one sphere, providing a sense of belonging and collective purpose. This sense of community extends into every aspect of life, including the world of trading, where the journey from beginner to expert can often feel like a one man journey. However, trading doesn't have to be a singular road to success, it can be a collaborative dedication while enriching experience when shared with others.

In India, where relationships and networks hold immense significance, being part of a trading community or having a mentor can make a huge difference in one's trading journey and to shape their mindset. These communities serve as the ultimate hubs of knowledge exchange, where traders of all levels come together to share experiences, strategies, and support each other through ups and downs of a functioning market. Whether it's discussing market trends, analyzing charts, or words of encouragement, the sense of companionship within these communities can provide invaluable motivation and guidance.

Take, for example, the thriving trading community in Mumbai, where traders gather regularly to discuss market developments and share insights. From seasoned professionals to eager learners, traders of all backgrounds come together to learn from one another and support each other's growth. Through introduction of various workshops, seminars, and online forums, the community fosters a spirit of collaborative helping hands and mutual respect. Empowering its members to navigate the complexities of the market with confidence and clarity.

But it's not just about sharing knowledge it's also about providing emotional support during the ups and downs of trading. The markets can be disruptive at times, testing even the most seasoned traders' experience. In these moments of uncleared path, having a supportive community to lean on can make all the difference, providing a safe space to vent discouragement and frustrations. You can seek advice, and celebrate victories together.

Indeed, the positive impact of trading communities on their members cannot be over exaggerated. Beyond the practical benefits of knowledge sharing and networking, these communities offer a sense of belonging and camaraderie that is invaluable in the often isolating world of trading. They remind us that we are not alone in our journey, that there are others who understand the challenges we face. Many are there for us to offer support and encourage us every step of the way.

By fostering this particular sense of community and social support, trading becomes more than just a means to financial success giving us the hype of relationships that we can build to rely on at times. It becomes a shared victory and a collective journey towards personal and professional growth. It's about lifting each other up, learning from one another's successes and failures, and ultimately, realizing our full potential as traders and as individuals. If you possibly skip this step your journey and growth might look way different.

In the context of Indian traders, where community and social connections are deeply appreciated and depended upon in the cultural fabric, the importance of trading communities cannot be overstated. By highlighting successful Indian trading communities and the positive impact they have on their members, this chapter aims to connect deeply with Indian traders, reflecting their unique aspirations, challenges, and cultural context to exponentially grow.

Section - 2
Directing the Mental Strata of Emotions

2.1 The Illusion of Get Rich Quick: Exposing the Myth of Easy Money

The idea of making quick money through trading has been highly romanticized, much like the blockbuster success stories in Bollywood. It's tempting to believe that the stock market is a magic portal to instant wealth and financial freedom. Many of us dream of making a fortune overnight, inspired by tales of sudden riches and the allure of living a life free from financial worries. However, the reality is far from this dream. Trading isn't a shortcut to wealth; it's a long-term journey requiring dedication, knowledge, and discipline.

In India, there is often a misconception that trading is akin to gambling—a game of chance where luck determines winners and losers. This perception is partly fueled by stories of people who seemingly struck gold without much effort. However, seasoned traders know that such success is not about luck but about having the right strategy, a solid understanding of the markets, and effective risk management.

Take the story of Rajesh, a young trader from Delhi. Enticed by the promise of easy money, Rajesh jumped into the stock market with dreams of quick riches. He had little understanding of trading principles and was driven by the hope of doubling his money overnight. Unfortunately, the market didn't align with his expectations. Rajesh soon faced significant losses, his savings dwindled, and his confidence shattered. This harsh lesson taught him that success in trading requires much more than hope and luck.

Stories like Rajesh's are common and serve as important reminders of the pitfalls of entering the market without proper preparation. Many people underestimate the effort and learning required to succeed in trading. The journey to becoming a successful trader is not smooth but filled with challenges that offer valuable lessons.

One major reason why many fall for the myth of easy money is the influence of readily available information. In today's digital age, information is just a click away, and the promise of quick profits is often hard to resist. However, trading is not about making quick decisions based on incomplete information. It's about patience and making informed choices.

The myth of easy money in trading is just that—a myth. While trading can be profitable, it demands hard work, persistence, and a commitment to learning from every experience. Only by approaching trading with a humble attitude, discipline, and a desire for continuous improvement can one hope to navigate the complexities of the market and achieve success.

To wrap up this chapter, it's essential to understand that the psychology of trading plays a critical role in determining outcomes. Emotions such as greed, fear, and overconfidence can cloud our judgment and lead to poor decisions. In the next chapter, we'll explore these emotions in more detail and discuss how to manage them effectively to maintain clarity and discipline in your trading journey.

2.2 Merging Emotions: Fright to Greed Displayed

In the bustling world of Indian financial markets, trading is a delicate dance between making practical decisions and navigating a sea of ever-changing emotions. Among these emotions, fright (fear) and greed are two of the most potent forces that can lead traders astray, often resulting in impulsive and unwise trading choices.

Fright: The Unseen Enemy

Fear in trading often springs from the uncertainty and volatility of the markets. It manifests in several ways that can undermine a trader's performance. One common scenario is the premature exit from trades. When the market experiences a downturn or sudden volatility, fear can prompt traders to hastily close their positions to prevent further losses. This reaction occurs even when the initial rationale behind the trade remains valid. As a result, traders might miss out on potential profits if the market eventually rebounds in the anticipated direction.

Fear can also deter traders from taking necessary risks. The anxiety of losing money or making a wrong move can paralyze decision-making, causing traders to miss out on promising opportunities. This aversion to risk can prevent traders from entering trades that offer favorable risk-reward ratios, ultimately capping their profit potential.

Greed: The Lure of More

On the flip side, greed is driven by an intense desire to maximize profits. This powerful emotion can push traders to overtrade and take on excessive risks.

After a series of winning trades, traders might become overconfident and stray from their trading plan, chasing after even greater gains. This can lead them to increase their position sizes or enter trades that don't align with their expertise or strategy. Such reckless risk-taking can wipe out previous profits and potentially devastate their trading portfolio.

Navigating Emotional Currents

To avoid the pitfalls of fear and greed, traders must develop self-awareness and adopt strategies to manage these emotions effectively. One useful approach is mindfulness. By practicing mindful reflection daily, traders can learn to recognize their emotions without judgment. This awareness allows them to identify when fear or greed is influencing their decisions and choose to respond thoughtfully rather than react impulsively.

Additionally, having a well-defined trading plan with clear criteria for entering and exiting trades can help remove emotional biases from trading decisions. By sticking to established rules, traders can make more rational choices based on their objective analysis rather than their emotional impulses.

Risk management is also crucial in trading. By limiting the size of each trade relative to their total capital and using stop-loss orders to cap potential losses, traders can reduce the fear of significant drawdowns and stay grounded, even when fear or greed threatens to take over.

Maintaining a long-term perspective can further help traders manage short-term emotional swings. By focusing on the overall trajectory of their trading performance rather than the outcome of individual trades, traders can be more resilient in the face of setbacks and remain committed to their strategies. This mindset reduces the emotional impact of temporary losses and supports consistent execution of trading plans.

Conclusion

Fright and greed are powerful emotions that can greatly influence trading decisions, often leading to undesirable outcomes. In the dynamic landscape of Indian financial markets, developing self-awareness, implementing effective emotional management strategies, and adhering to disciplined trading practices are essential. By mastering these skills, traders can mitigate the impact of these emotions and make more rational, profitable decisions.

2.3 How Overconfidence Consumes You And Your Success

Have you ever imagined what your life could be like if you were free from all the obstacles holding you back from achieving your goals? Picture a life where setbacks no longer hinder your progress, where you live with unwavering confidence, navigating your journey without the fear of going astray. It sounds wonderful, doesn't it? But to reach this ideal, it's crucial to understand the fine line between confidence and overconfidence.

Confidence is the fuel that drives your growth and empowers you to advance steadily towards your dreams. However, overconfidence can be a deceptive force, filling you with excessive pride and leading you to take unnecessary risks without proper consideration. It's not that you shouldn't take risks, but there's a difference between calculated risks and reckless actions driven by overconfidence.

Confidence vs. Overconfidence

Consider two scenarios. In the first, imagine someone cultivating a new skill. They practice, learn from their mistakes, and build a solid foundation. They study the experiences of others, analyze the results, and strategically plan their next steps. When they finally take the leap, it's a calculated risk, informed by knowledge and preparation.

Now, imagine a beginner trader who, seeing a friend's success, jumps into the market without any prior experience or guidance. They rely on unreliable sources like "Learn to Trade in One Week" and make their first small profit. Overconfident from this initial success, they start making larger trades in unfamiliar markets. Inevitably, the market turns against them, and they lose all their capital. This is a harsh lesson in the dangers of overconfidence.

The Double-Edged Sword of Success

In trading, success can be both a blessing and a curse. Consistent gains might make you feel invincible, leading to a dangerous level of overconfidence. You start to believe you can tackle any challenge the market throws your way. But remember, being a "Jack of all trades and master of none" can lead you to overestimate your abilities and take unnecessary risks.

While confidence is essential for navigating the complex world of trading, unchecked overconfidence can erode your profits and endanger your financial stability. Let's explore how overconfidence can negatively impact your trading behavior and discuss strategies to stay grounded in the face of success.

The Delusion of Invincibility

Success breeds confidence, but without proper checks, it can morph into overconfidence. After a streak of profitable trades, some traders may start to believe they possess a special skill that sets them apart. This sense of invincibility can lead them to take on increasingly risky trades without adequate understanding or preparation. This can quickly backfire, resulting in significant losses.

Overtrading: The Lack of Patience

Overtrading is a common pitfall for the overconfident trader. Believing in their ability to outsmart the market, they might enter trades impulsively, without thorough analysis. This behavior can deplete their capital and erode their gains, leaving them worse off than when they started.

The Trap of Excessive Risk-Taking

Overconfident traders often fall into the trap of taking excessive risks. They might disregard risk management principles, convinced they can handle any market movement. What starts as a confident bet can quickly turn into a significant financial setback, causing emotional distress and financial loss.

Staying Grounded Amid Success

To avoid the dangers of overconfidence, it's essential to stay grounded. Here are some strategies to help maintain a balanced perspective:

1. **Cultivate Self-Awareness:** Regularly assess your trading behavior and mindset. Ask yourself: Are you becoming overly confident? Are you taking unnecessary risks? By reflecting on your actions, you can identify signs of overconfidence and make adjustments before costly mistakes occur.

2. **Stick to Your Trading Plan:** Develop a robust trading plan with clear entry and exit criteria and a solid risk management strategy. Commit to following this plan even when tempted to deviate. Consistency in adhering to your plan can prevent impulsive decisions driven by overconfidence.

3. **Diversify Your Portfolio:** Avoid putting all your capital into one type of trade. Diversify your investments across different assets to spread risk and

cushion against potential losses. Diversification fosters resilience and helps protect your portfolio from the impacts of overconfident trading.

4. **Seek Continuous Learning:** The financial markets are always evolving. Stay curious and committed to learning. Acknowledge that there is always more to understand and embrace a growth mindset. Invest in your education through books, courses, seminars, and mentorship from experienced traders. By prioritizing learning, you can avoid complacency and keep your skills sharp.

5. **Manage Your Emotions:** Emotional discipline is crucial in trading. Practice mindfulness techniques like deep breathing or meditation to stay calm during volatile market conditions. By managing your emotions, you can make rational decisions based on data and analysis rather than being swayed by overconfidence or fear.

Conclusion

Success in trading can be thrilling, but it carries the risk of breeding overconfidence. Without checks, overconfidence can lead to reckless behavior, excessive risk-taking, and significant financial losses. By cultivating self-awareness, sticking to a disciplined trading plan, diversifying your portfolio, and committing to continuous learning, you can maintain emotional balance and make sound trading decisions.

This chapter provides you with the tools to navigate the emotional challenges of trading. By understanding and managing overconfidence, you can achieve sustainable success and turn your trading dreams into reality. Remember, the journey to financial prosperity requires not just skill and strategy, but also a humble mindset and disciplined approach. Embrace these principles, and let them guide you to a future filled with endless possibilities

2.4 Guide You Through An Unstructured Roadmap Takes You To Failure

SIGNS OF AN UNSTRUCTURED TRADING PLAN:

1. Skipping the Pre-Trade Analysis

Beginning your trading practice without conducting a thorough pre-trade analysis is a minus. This means many understated negative outcomes. If you are neglecting to analyze market trends, condition of the market, important factors to take in consideration, and reasonable technical indicators before entering a trade. Missing all these rational steps and containing little to no market knowledge of the sectors you are trading in, will not give you an expected exit either. Without proper analysis it is impossible for traders to essentially make profits. So making informed decisions based on data and evidence is more reliable and relieving.

2. Overtrading

Overtrading occurs when traders get trapped into the greed of quick profits and eventually execute an excessive number of trades, often out of boredom, impulsiveness, or a desire to cover initial losses quickly. Overtrading is never not planned and it's often a category of an unstructured trading plan. This behavior can lead to hype in constant transactions, emotional exhaustion, and unvarying returns which significantly affect and demotivate a good profit streak. A disciplined approach that rather pays attention to quality over quantity is essential to avoid falling into the trap of overtrading.

3. Recklessly Covering Losses

Chasing losses made in the past is a common mistake among traders. And many times there's a trader who refuses to accept defeat and an impulsive mindset borne by it leads to the trader losing his position and profits on a daily basis. They might double down on losing positions in the hope of reversing their fortunes but the search for such 'recovering fortunes' ends up blinding the trader and they instantly get hit by a rock reality. This often leads to further losses with each try to get covered in an impulsive hope and causes emotional distress. Successful traders understand the importance of cutting losses quickly and they prefer moving on to the next opportunity rather than affecting themselves due to past failures.

4. Ignoring Risk-Reward Ratios

Trading without considering the possibility of risk-reward ratios is a path down for disaster. By following this step, a favorable risk-reward ratio ensures that potential profits outdo the potential losses, providing a protection against adverse market movements and drawbacks. Ignoring and avoiding this fundamental principle that can cover your risk optimally. Lack of practices like these can expose beginner to seasoned traders to unnecessary risk and majorly affect their long-term profitability.

5. Emotional Trading

Emotions have no place in a path to successful trading, despite this many traders let fear, greed, and anxiety slide into making their decisions on a subconscious basis. Emotional ways of trading and letting your inner thought take over your psyche's analysis can often result in impulsive decisions, unreasonable behavior, and indicates very poor judgment skills. Developing emotional consideration, resilience, and maintaining a calm, practical mindset are essential for staying focused, disciplined and efficient in the face of market unreliability.

6. Lack of Journaling and Review

As a trader the utmost practice you can learn is to keep a trading journal to regularly review your performances in the past trades and highlighting the key indicators that helped to overcome the mistake. Being self aware about all the possible drawbacks you might face can be a hit opportunity for learning and improvement. Furthermore, you will consider all the mistakes you made which led to impulsive and negative outcomes affecting your progress. While journaling allows traders to track their past performance and improve in the future, identify patterns, and recognize areas for growth and without such feedback, traders are more likely to get stuck in a loop and repeat the same mistakes and struggle to progress in their trading journey.

7. No Clear Exit Strategy

Whenever you enter a trade ask yourself one question- "What is the motive of this trade I'm entering and outcome I want out of this trade?"

Recklessly entering trades without a clear exit strategy is a sign of unstructured trading practice. A well-defined and targeted exit strategy should outline specific criteria's for closing out positions with executed risks. Whether it's based on reaching profit targets, trailing stop-loss orders, or changes in market conditions. Without a clear plan for exiting trades and proper execution, traders risk holding onto losing positions for too long and might be missing out on potential profits.

In the world of trading, success isn't just about making the right decisions; it's also about testing yourself on how good you are at avoiding common pitfalls that can break down even the most promising strategies.

Two extremely critical areas where traders often startle themselves are the lack of a solid trading foundation or plan and inadequate risk management system. Let's delve into these essential aspects possibly affecting your growth. Let's understand why it is inevitable to practice in order to achieve sustainable success in the volatile markets.

THE NECESSITIES AND WAYS OF BUILDING A WELL-DEFINED TRADING PLAN:

Imagine setting out on a long journey without a map or a destination in mind. Do you think it's possible to be so spontaneous? Unless you're ready to face the repercussions of your actions. You wouldn't know where you're going or how to get there. Likewise, trading without a well-defined plan means navigating the markets blindly without any reliable basis and resources to reach your goal. A trading plan serves as your roadmap, providing clarity and direction in the often chaotic world of trading.

1. Clear Objectives

A trading plan begins with clearly defining your objectives and motives. What are your goals as a trader? Are you looking to generate consistent income, invest while growing your capital steadily, or achieve specific and planned financial milestones? By establishing clear objectives, you can tailor your trading approach to align with your goals.

2. Defining Entry and Exit Points

This point is one of the most non negotiable components of a trading plan. To define and execute precise entry and exit points. This involves identifying favorable opportunities where you can get a leeway to enter trades swiftly based on your technical analysis and risk criteria of the particular sector. It is also equally important to determine when to exit those trades, as a trader you should be well aware of the possible risk factors hindering your profitable position. Does not matter whether it's to lock in profits or cut losses before they escalate. Only thing to make sure that the leap of losses is not affecting significantly on your progress.

3. Implementing Risk Management Strategies

Effective risk management is at the heart of a sincere and robust trading plan. It involves entering into the potential risks associated with each trade. This includes determining the appropriate position size, setting strategies for stop-loss orders to limit losses potentially, and striving to diversify your portfolio to spread risk across different assets. Again

4. Maintaining Discipline and Consistency

Perhaps the most challenging aspect of trading is maintaining discipline and consistency. Building and creating routine A well-defined trading plan acts as a safeguard against emotional decision-making and impulsive actions. It provides a structured framework that helps you stick to your strategy even when faced with market volatility or uncertainty.

MISTAKES MADE- STRATEGIES FOR EFFECTIVE RISK MANAGEMENT

While having a trading plan is essential, it's equally important to implement effective risk management strategies to safeguard your capital. Let's explore some common risk management mistakes and practical advice for avoiding them.

1. Risking Too Much on a Single Trade

One of the most common pitfalls traders encounter is risking too much capital on a single trade. While it can be tempting to go all-in on a promising opportunity, doing so can expose you to significant losses if the trade goes against you. This might also develop as a habit. Instead, resort to the principle of never risking more than a small percentage of your trading capital on any single trade to make sure that even if you make a loss you can cover or bear that.

2. Neglecting Stop-Loss Orders

Stop-loss orders are a vital tool for managing risk and cutting losses, yet many traders overlook them. These orders allow you to set predefined rules and exit points for your trades, ensuring that losses are kept within acceptable limits and do not hurt your progress. Don't think of it as a rule but make it a habit to always use stop-loss orders and adjust them as the trade progresses to protect your capital.

3. Regularly Review and Adjust

Risk management is not a one-time task and a once in a blue moon activity. You need to perpetually activate the habit. In an ongoing process like trading which is practiced on most days by traders, it is necessary to be regular with review and essential adjustments. Over time, spread your knowledge and evaluate your trading plan and risk management strategies to ensure they remain aligned with your objectives and market conditions. Be prepared to make changes as needed to adapt to evolving circumstances.

Conclusion

In the world of trading, success is not easy and guaranteed, but it is based on your efforts to thrive on your experiences and make a well-defined trading plan by implementing effective risk management strategies that can significantly increase your odds of success. By setting clear objectives, defining entry and exit points, and managing risk skillfully, you can navigate the markets with confidence and consistency and further you will be able to master it to such an extent that your predictions won't be needed to rectify with time consuming analysis. Remember, trading is as much about mindset, patience, discipline and learning through the way as it is about analysis and strategy. Stay disciplined and always prioritize the protection of your capital and don't be impulsive and reckless by unreliable ways of profits blinding you.

2.5 Building a Seasoned Mindset Before Becoming a Trader: Overcoming Analysis Paralysis and Cultivating Psychological Resilience

In the dynamic world of trading, success hinges not only on your ability to analyze the markets but also on your mental fortitude and emotional control. This chapter delves into the intertwined challenges of analysis paralysis and the necessity for psychological resilience. We offer practical insights and techniques tailored for the Indian audience aiming to enhance their trading skills and mindset.

Navigating the Sea of Information

In today's digital age, traders are bombarded with an overwhelming amount of information—from market news and technical indicators to varying perspectives from countless experts. It's easy to become paralyzed by the sheer volume of data, leading to indecision and hesitation. This phenomenon, known as analysis paralysis, is particularly common among Indian traders, where the surge in interest in stock trading and investing has been fueled by the explosion of online resources and trading platforms.

To combat analysis paralysis, Indian traders should adopt a focused and disciplined approach to technical analysis. Instead of trying to digest every piece of information, it's crucial to prioritize key indicators and trends that align with your trading strategy and goals. This might involve using technical tools like candlestick patterns, moving averages, and support/resistance levels, complemented by fundamental analysis that considers economic factors and company performance.

Creating a structured trading plan with clear entry and exit criteria can also provide clarity and direction, especially during periods of market uncertainty. By defining specific trading rules and risk management strategies, traders can reduce the fear of making wrong decisions and boost their confidence in executing trades effectively.

Embracing the Psychological Dimension

While technical analysis is essential for understanding market dynamics, mastering the psychological aspects of trading is equally crucial for long-term success. In India, where attitudes towards risk-taking and financial markets vary widely, managing one's psychological state is key to navigating the emotional highs and lows of trading.

Ignoring the psychological component can lead to emotional turbulence, where fear, greed, and anxiety dictate your trading decisions. To build mental resilience, Indian traders must first recognize and acknowledge their emotional triggers and biases. This self-awareness is the foundation for developing effective strategies to maintain emotional balance, even during volatile market conditions.

Practical techniques such as mindfulness meditation, deep breathing, and visualization can help traders stay calm and centered amid market chaos. Additionally, connecting with a community of like-minded traders through online forums or local trading groups can provide invaluable emotional support and camaraderie.

By integrating psychological resilience with technical analysis, Indian traders can navigate market complexities with greater confidence and stability. Continuous self-reflection and awareness foster a sharp mindset that enhances trading performance and promotes overall well-being and fulfillment.

Overcoming Analysis Paralysis

1. **Focus on Key Indicators:** Identify and concentrate on a few critical technical indicators that align with your trading strategy. This focused approach helps streamline your analysis and avoids overwhelming you with too much information.

2. **Set Clear Objectives:** Define your trading goals and align your analysis with these objectives. Whether it's short-term gains or long-term growth, having clear goals will help guide your analysis and decision-making.

3. **Create a Trading Plan:** Develop a detailed trading plan that includes your entry and exit points, risk management strategies, and criteria for making trades. A well-structured plan reduces the chances of analysis paralysis by providing a clear roadmap for your trading activities.

4. **Limit Your Data Sources:** Stick to a few reliable sources of information and avoid the temptation to consult too many. This will help you stay focused and avoid getting bogged down by conflicting data.

Cultivating Psychological Resilience

1. **Recognize Emotional Triggers:** Pay attention to what causes emotional reactions in your trading. Understanding your triggers can help you develop strategies to manage them effectively.

2. **Practice Mindfulness:** Incorporate mindfulness techniques such as meditation or deep breathing into your routine. These practices can help you stay calm and focused, even in volatile market conditions.

3. **Build a Support Network:** Engage with other traders who share your goals and experiences. A supportive community can provide encouragement, share insights, and help you stay grounded.

4. **Stay Disciplined:** Stick to your trading plan and avoid making impulsive decisions based on emotions. Consistency and discipline are key to maintaining psychological resilience.

Conclusion

Mastering the trader's mindset is a continuous journey that requires balancing analytical acumen with psychological strength. By overcoming analysis paralysis and embracing the psychological challenges of trading, Indian traders can unlock their full potential and pave the way toward financial security and personal growth. Remember, success in trading is not just about understanding the markets; it's also about mastering your mind and emotions to make thoughtful, informed decisions that lead to long-term success.

2.6 The Cons of Falling for Trading Myths: A Way Out for Indian Traders

In the vast and ever-evolving landscape of India's financial markets, traders often find themselves ensnared by myths, misconceptions, and overblown hype.

These myths can create a maze that traps traders, leading them to make poor decisions if they lack proper guidance. While staying informed is crucial for making sound trading decisions, the dangers of relying on trading myths cannot be overstated. This chapter highlights the pitfalls of falling for these myths and offers practical strategies tailored for Indian traders to navigate through the noise and find clarity.

Myths: The Power of Easy Influence

In the bustling world of trading, where fortunes can be made or lost in seconds, the allure of trading myths is incredibly strong. Stories of overnight riches and whispers of foolproof strategies can tempt traders into believing in quick gains. However, beneath this tempting facade lies a complex web of risks and pitfalls that can ensnare even experienced traders.

The Pitfalls of Unverified Information

One of the biggest dangers of trading myths is the reliance on unverified information. In India, where the number of retail investors in the stock market has surged, traders are particularly vulnerable to misinformation spread through social media, WhatsApp groups, and sensationalized news. Acting on such unverified information without conducting thorough analysis can lead to poorly informed decisions and significant financial losses.

The Importance of Independent Research

To navigate the treacherous waters of trading myths, Indian traders must prioritize independent research and critical thinking. It's crucial not to get swept up by the herd mentality or the fear of missing out (FOMO). Traders should adopt a disciplined approach to gathering and analyzing information. This includes cross-referencing multiple sources, verifying the credibility of news outlets and analysts, and conducting deep fundamental and technical analysis before making any trading decisions.

Relying on Credible Sources

In an age of information overload, distinguishing between credible sources and sensationalized news is vital. Indian traders should prioritize reputable financial news outlets, regulatory filings, and analytic reports when seeking market insights. Additionally, seeking guidance from trusted mentors, industry experts, and experienced traders can provide invaluable perspectives and help navigate the complexities of the market.

Maintaining a Skeptical Mindset

While staying informed is essential, Indian traders must cultivate a healthy skepticism towards trading myths and rumors. Questioning the motives behind sensational headlines and examining the validity of market-moving events can serve as a defense against misinformation. By fostering a rational and analytical mindset, traders can shield themselves from herd mentality and make well-informed decisions based on objective analysis.

Common Misconceptions Hindering Trader Growth

1. **Insider Trading Always Pays Off:** There's a widespread belief that trading on insider information guarantees profits. However, acting on insider tips is illegal and can result in severe penalties, regardless of how lucrative it may seem.

2. **Trading in Penny Stocks Equals Great Profits:** Many believe that investing in low-priced penny stocks will lead to huge returns. However, penny stocks are often highly volatile and speculative, carrying significant risks that can outweigh potential gains.

3. **Following the Crowd Guarantees Success:** Some traders think that following popular trends or the herd will lead to success. However, this can lead to buying at inflated prices and selling during downturns, resulting in losses.

4. **Day Trading is a Quick Path to Wealth:** Day trading, or buying and selling within the same day, is often glamorized as a way to get rich quickly.

In reality, it requires skill, discipline, and effective risk management, and many day traders end up incurring losses.

5. **Technical Analysis is the Only Key:** While technical analysis is valuable, relying solely on it can be misleading. Market dynamics are influenced by various factors, and incorporating both technical and fundamental analysis is crucial for informed decision-making.

6. **Timing the Market:** The idea of perfectly timing the market—buying low and selling high—is virtually impossible. Market timing strategies often fail because of the market's inherent volatility and unpredictability.

7. **Investing in IPOs Guarantees Profits:** Initial Public Offerings (IPOs) are often hyped as quick money-makers. However, IPOs can be volatile, and not all newly public companies succeed in the long term. Careful research and analysis are necessary.

8. **Diversification is Overrated:** Some traders think that concentrating investments in a few stocks is the key to maximizing returns. However, lack of diversification increases risk, as adverse events can disproportionately impact their portfolio.

9. **Fundamental Analysis is Outdated:** With the rise of algorithmic trading and technical analysis tools, some dismiss fundamental analysis as old-fashioned. However, assessing a company's financial health and performance remains crucial for making sound investment decisions.

10. **Trading Requires High Capital:** There's a misconception that successful trading requires substantial capital. While more capital provides more opportunities, it's possible to start with smaller amounts and focus on sound risk management and strategy execution.

Conclusion: Defeat the Lies

In conclusion, trading myths present a significant challenge for Indian traders striving to navigate the complexities of the financial markets. By recognizing the pitfalls of unverified information and emphasizing independent research, traders can protect their portfolios and manage the risks associated with these myths. Through disciplined analysis, critical thinking, and a confident approach to debunking misinformation, Indian traders can pave the way to sustained success and financial prosperity.

These myths underscore the importance of thorough research, maintaining a disciplined routine, and honing your mental acumen. Seeking reliable sources and verifying information are crucial steps in protecting yourself from the dangers of trading myths. In the next section, we'll explore how to cultivate a winning mindset and train your mind to resist undue influence, ensuring your trading journey is guided by clarity and purpose.

Section - 3
Planting A Winning Mindset

3.1 Path to Consistent Success

In the high-stakes world of trading, success isn't just about analyzing charts and making the right predictions. It's also about developing a winning mindset that ensures you make well-controlled decisions. In this chapter, we'll explore practical strategies to build the mental strength and resilience needed to succeed in the ever-changing markets. We've previously discussed risk management and setting clear goals; now, we'll focus on strengthening our minds to face decisions with confidence and courage. This section will provide you with tools to build a robust trading plan and navigate the market's ups and downs confidently.

1. Understanding the Power of the Mind

Before diving into trading strategies, it's crucial to understand how powerful your mindset is in determining your trading success. Your beliefs, attitudes, and emotions can greatly influence your decisions, ultimately deciding your success or failure as a trader.

Think of your mind as a powerful tool— it can either be your greatest ally or your biggest enemy. Regularly talking to yourself and keeping a journal can help you understand how your mind works in your case. Ask yourself these questions and write down the answers:

- Is my mind helping or hindering me?
- Do I often feel confused or indecisive?
- Am I making decisions at the right time?

By understanding your mental patterns, you can start to harness the power of your mind to make better trading decisions.

2. Building a Winning Mindset

Developing a Robust Trading Plan

A successful trader's journey starts with a well-defined trading plan. This plan is your blueprint for success and includes clear entry and exit points, risk management rules, and both short-term and long-term goals. A structured plan helps you avoid impulsive decisions and maintain consistency in your trading approach, reducing stress and increasing confidence.

Here's how to build a stress-free trading routine:

- **Entry and Exit Points:** Define clear criteria for when to enter and exit trades based on thorough analysis and technical indicators. Stick to rational decisions, not emotional impulses.

- **Risk Management Rules:** Decide how much risk you can tolerate per trade and overall. Always use stop-loss orders to protect your capital.

- **Trading Goals:** Set specific, measurable goals to keep yourself motivated and focused on long-term success. While setting limits, keep a mindset of boundless potential.

- **Review and Adaptation:** Regularly review your trading plan and make necessary adjustments based on your performance and changing market conditions. Always look for ways to improve and adapt

3. Maintaining Discipline and Patience

Consistent discipline and patience are key virtues for successful traders. It's easy to get caught up in the excitement of potential profits, especially when a previous strategy has worked well. But the market's volatility can easily trap you into making impulsive decisions. True success requires a calm, disciplined approach to your trading actions.

- **Sticking to Your Plan:** Resist the urge to deviate from your trading plan, even during uncertainty or market volatility. Sometimes, greed or the lure of quick profits can tempt traders to stray from their plan.

- **Practicing Patience**: Remember, Rome wasn't built in a day, and neither is a successful trading career. Be patient and trust the process, knowing that success comes with time and dedication. Just like a boxer studies his opponent's moves to anticipate and counter them, you should learn to read market patterns and act wisely.

4. Embracing Continuous Learning

Markets are always evolving, and staying up-to-date is crucial. Successful traders are always ready to learn from their experiences and adapt for the future. Whether it's keeping up with market trends, improving your technical skills, or seeking mentorship, continuous learning is essential. Each day, strive to be better than you were yesterday.

- **Stay Informed**: Keep yourself updated on the latest market news and developments that could impact your trading decisions.
- **Invest in Education**: Take courses, read books, and attend seminars to

deepen your understanding of trading strategies and techniques. Explore new areas to expand your knowledge and skills.

- **Seek Feedback**: Join a community of traders you can rely on for advice and feedback. Surround yourself with supportive individuals, either online or in person, who can help you grow and provide valuable insights.

5. Finding the Win in Every Loss

One of the most important lessons in trading is finding the win in every loss. Trading isn't just about making money; it's also about personal growth. By seeing failure as an opportunity for learning, traders can turn setbacks into steps toward success.

- **Embracing Failure**: Don't dwell on losses. Use them as learning experiences to identify areas for improvement and refine your strategy. Treat each failure as a lesson to grow from.

- **Maintaining Perspective**: Remember that trading is a marathon, not a sprint. Focus on steady, long-term progress rather than short-term gains. Avoid taking large, risky leaps that could jeopardize your success.
- **Cultivating Gratitude**: Celebrate each win with gratitude. This practice keeps you humble and driven for long-term success. Reflect daily on your growth and the lessons learned from both successes and failures

Conclusion:

In the fast-paced world of trading, a winning mindset often makes the difference between success and failure. By understanding the power of the mind, developing a strong trading plan, and seeing failure as a step towards success, traders can build the resilience and mental strength needed to thrive in the markets. Let's embark on this journey together and master the mindset of a successful trader.

3.2 The Ultimate Power of Visualization

Harnessing the power of visualization offers a robust method for Indian traders to enhance their trading performance. In the dynamic world of trading, where mental and emotional factors play a crucial role in decision-making, visualization can serve as a powerful tool. By mentally rehearsing successful trades and visualizing desired outcomes, traders can condition their minds to stay focused and disciplined, even amidst the market's volatility.

In a rapidly growing market like India, where conditions can change quickly, the power of visualization helps maintain composure and fosters rational decision-making, even in high-pressure situations. Creating a vision board or regularly practicing visualization can boost your confidence in your trading strategies and goals. Remember, your mental capability determines how well you can handle challenges. When facing tough situations, it's not just You versus You; it's You versus The Problem.

Building Confidence and Self-Belief

For Indian traders, building and sustaining confidence is not just a task but a transformative journey. The market landscape often shifts due to external factors like political events, economic policies, and global trends, making it challenging to overcome self-doubt.

Indian traders can draw strength from their rich cultural heritage, which offers wisdom through ancient scriptures and modern philosophies. These teachings emphasize self-awareness, resilience, and the power of belief. Integrating these principles into your daily practices can help build unshakeable confidence.

Reflect on your past achievements, no matter how small they may seem. Celebrate these victories as they are stepping stones to greater success. Tracking your growth and acknowledging how far you've come can boost your self-belief and resilience. Indian traders can use these reflections as a foundation to build confidence and to face challenges with a stronger mindset.

Incorporating positive affirmations rooted in Indian philosophies can also be a powerful tool. Reciting mantras or embracing teachings from revered sages can serve as constant reminders of your inner strength and potential. Many in India believe in the power of manifesting progress through daily affirmations. Once you convince yourself of your inherent power, no obstacle can hold you back.

Additionally, engaging with supportive trading communities is vital for building confidence. Surrounding yourself with like-minded individuals who offer companionship and encouragement can greatly enhance your trading knowledge and provide emotional support during tough times.

In essence, building and sustaining confidence involves drawing from cultural wisdom, celebrating personal wins, embracing positive affirmations, and engaging with supportive communities. By integrating these elements into their trading journey, Indian traders can develop strong self-belief and navigate market complexities with unwavering confidence.

Embracing Adaptability and Flexibility

The Indian market is known for its exclusivity and unpredictability, requiring a high degree of adaptability and flexibility among traders. Each person has their own pace of learning and adaptation. It's important to acknowledge that while it may take time to master a new ability, the speed at which you adapt can be crucial.

Some traders might hesitate due to a lack of adaptability, but it's essential to embrace this trait because everyone's journey is unique. In trading, no two players have the same role, and it's this diversity that makes the market dynamic and exciting. Embrace your unique learning path and express it confidently.

Strategies that worked in the past may need to be adjusted or even completely restructured to align with new market conditions. Staying informed about geopolitical developments, regulatory changes, and sector-specific trends is crucial for Indian traders. Flexibility in mindset and approach allows you to quickly adjust to market shifts, capitalize on emerging opportunities, and minimize risks.

Cultivating a culture of continuous learning and experimentation enables Indian traders to stay ahead of market trends and maintain a competitive edge in the ever-evolving marketplace.

Building Emotional Intelligence

Emotional intelligence is critical for Indian traders dealing with the market's complexities. Managing emotions like fear, greed, and uncertainty is essential. Many traders develop a fear of changing strategies as the market changes, but developing self-awareness helps you recognize emotional triggers and implement strategies to regulate responses effectively.

In India, family and societal expectations can add extra pressure on traders. Practicing mindfulness and self-care is crucial for maintaining emotional balance and mental well-being. Cultivating empathy towards fellow traders fosters a sense of connection and mutual understanding, laying the foundation for collaborative relationships and collective growth.

By prioritizing emotional intelligence, traders can enhance their decision-making abilities and build resilience in the face of adverse market conditions, leading to sustainable success and fulfillment.

Integrating Trading Psychology into Practice

To master the art of trading psychology, Indian traders must integrate these principles into their daily routines. This involves incorporating visualization exercises, confidence-building techniques, adaptive strategies, and emotional intelligence practices into their trading plans.

Leverage the vast amount of data available online, including YouTube and other social media platforms, to grow your mindset. Study yourself and each step you take. Reflect on every mistake and decision. Understanding how your mind controls you is key to avoiding stress and staying focused.

Keep a trading journal to track your thoughts, emotions, and outcomes. This practice provides valuable insights into your patterns and behaviors, facilitating continuous improvement and self-discovery. Use online resources, but remember, no one knows you better than yourself. Document every change and new learning about yourself. Every small step matters, just like every action in trading.

Seeking mentorship from seasoned traders or participating in formal training programs focused on trading psychology can offer valuable guidance and support. By embracing trading psychology as a core part of their journey, Indian traders can cultivate resilience, adaptability, and emotional intelligence, positioning themselves for long-term success in the dynamic marketplace.

Conclusion

As Indian traders navigate the complexities of the market, mastering trading psychology is crucial for achieving sustainable success and fulfillment. By harnessing the power of visualization, building strong confidence, embracing adaptability, and honing emotional intelligence, traders can tackle challenges with clarity and seize opportunities confidently. By committing to these principles, Indian traders can unlock their full potential and thrive in the vibrant market landscape, turning their aspirations into reality and setting a winning mindset for future opportunities.

3.3 Setting Yourself Up for the Long-Term

In the world of trading, success isn't a short-lived trend that fades away in a few months. It requires ongoing effort, continuous learning, and a commitment to a sustainable lifestyle. Imagine building a house: you can't just lay the foundation and expect it to stand forever. You need to keep working on it, maintaining and upgrading it over time. Similarly, in trading, you need to keep growing, adapting, and refining your approach. If you get too satisfied with small successes, you risk losing the reputation and progress you've made. To be truly successful in the long run, you need resilience, patience, and a clear purpose guiding your actions.

Balancing Ambition and Contentment

In the realm of trading, balancing ambition and contentment is about finding a middle path between striving for success and being satisfied with your achievements. Ambition drives traders to set high financial goals, seek out profitable opportunities, and take calculated risks to maximize returns. It pushes you to keep analyzing markets, developing new strategies, and aiming for growth.

However, unchecked ambition, where you have too many goals without a clear plan, can lead to excessive risk-taking, overtrading, and stress. It creates a mindset where success is measured only by financial gains, leaving you feeling unsatisfied even with significant profits.

This relentless pursuit of more can make you overlook what you already have, neglecting the importance of preserving capital and managing risks effectively.

On the flip side, contentment in trading means appreciating the journey and being grateful for your achievements, no matter how small. It's about finding joy in the process of trading itself—the intellectual challenge, the freedom, and the autonomy. Contentment also means having peace and balance, where you're not always chasing the next big win but enjoying a consistent, sustainable approach to trading.

Finding the right balance between ambition and contentment requires a thoughtful approach. Traders should set ambitious yet realistic goals, aiming for growth while understanding the risks and uncertainties of the market. Cultivating a mindset of continuous improvement without losing sight of patience, discipline, and resilience is key. Practicing gratitude and mindfulness regularly, reflecting on your achievements, and remembering why you started trading can help you stay grounded and focused.

Success in trading should enhance both your professional and personal life. By balancing ambition and contentment, you can navigate the market's complexities with resilience, clarity, and peace of mind, leading to long-term success and prosperity. For Indian traders, this balance is essential for sustaining motivation and progress. Setting realistic goals and appreciating what you have fosters a harmonious blend of ambition and contentment on your journey toward excellence.

Embracing Change and Innovation

In trading, embracing change and innovation is crucial for staying ahead. The Indian market, like others, constantly evolves with new technologies, strategies, and trends. Being open to these changes and fostering a mindset of curiosity and experimentation is vital. This openness allows traders to adapt, innovate, and remain competitive in the ever-changing Indian trading environment.

Grabbing each opportunity that comes your way, while being open to new ideas and technologies, positions you for success. Whether it's adopting the latest trading tools, exploring new market strategies, or staying informed about market trends, embracing change and innovation keeps you ahead of the curve.

Conclusion

As Indian traders embark on their journey toward excellence, mastering the mindset is crucial for achieving sustained success and fulfillment. By fostering a growth mindset, practicing gratitude and positivity, balancing ambition and contentment, and embracing change and innovation, traders can navigate the market's complexities with resilience and passion. This approach positions them for success and abundance in the dynamic Indian trading landscape.

With a steadfast commitment to developing the right mindset, Indian traders can turn challenges into opportunities, achieve greatness in the trading world, and set themselves apart from the crowd. The path to long-term success in trading is paved with continuous growth, self-reflection, and the courage to embrace change.

In the next chapter, we'll delve into the destination of success and the psychology behind winning in the markets. The journey towards mastering trading and achieving your goals continues...

Section - 4
Begin To Not Put An End

4.1 Traders' Initial Journey and Breakthrough

Many people start their trading journey with a burst of enthusiasm, often inspired by flashy Instagram reels or stories of quick success. However, there's a significant difference between being motivated to make money and being motivated to learn the art of trading. This chapter explores the initial phase of most traders' journeys and why many fail to continue beyond the first year.

The Initial Rush

When traders first dive into the market, they often do so with high hopes and expectations. It's not uncommon for new traders to see some early success, making quick profits and feeling the rush of excitement. This initial success can be intoxicating, leading them to believe that trading is an easy path to wealth. However, this honeymoon phase is often short-lived.

Statistics and Reality

According to statistics, 60% of people quit trading, and 70% give up within the first year. Why does this happen? The answer lies in the unrealistic expectations set during the initial phase. Early profits create a false sense of security and inflate expectations. Traders begin to think that continuous gains are guaranteed and overlook the inherent volatility of the market.

The Downfall

As traders progress, they inevitably encounter losses. The market's unpredictable nature starts to show its true colors. Many traders, having been lulled into a false sense of security, are unprepared for these downturns. They become hesitant, fearful, and often overwhelmed when the market doesn't behave as they expected.

The real challenge in trading is not making initial profits but learning to navigate the inevitable setbacks. This is where most traders falter. They fail to understand that losses are a natural part of the trading journey. Instead of viewing setbacks as learning opportunities, they see them as failures, leading to frustration and the eventual decision to quit.

Testing Your Resilience

The market is like a stormy sea, constantly testing the resilience of those who venture into its waters. The question isn't whether you will face challenges but how you will respond when they arise. Will you let setbacks define you, or will you use them as stepping stones to growth?

To succeed in trading, you need to develop the patience to endure tough times and the strength to learn from them. You must give the market time to test you and prove your resilience. Many traders fail because they don't allow themselves the opportunity to grow through adversity. They quit before discovering their true potential.

The Importance of Learning

Continuous learning is the key to long-term success in trading. The market is ever-changing, and the strategies that worked yesterday may not work tomorrow. To stay ahead, you need to keep learning, adapting, and refining your approach. This means embracing both your successes and your failures as opportunities for growth.

It's important to remember that every setback is a chance to learn and improve. When you hit a rough patch, take a step back and analyze what went wrong. Adjust your strategy, refine your plan, and move forward with renewed focus. This process of perpetual learning and adaptation is what separates successful traders from those who give up.

Finding Your Breakthrough

Every trader's journey is unique, and breakthroughs come at different times for everyone. Some may find success quickly, while others may struggle for years before hitting their stride. The key is to stay committed, keep learning, and never give up.

Your breakthrough will come when you least expect it. It could be a moment of clarity during a tough market day or a gradual realization of your growing skills and confidence. When it happens, you'll understand that the struggles and setbacks were all part of the journey, shaping you into a stronger, more resilient trader.

If You're Feeling Stuck

If you find yourself stuck in any phase of your trading journey, my advice is simple: Stay the course. The market is a test of endurance as much as it is of skill. It's about how long you can hold on and keep pushing forward despite the challenges.

Remember, success in trading is not about never failing; it's about learning to pick yourself up each time you do. The market rewards those who have the patience to weather the storms and the tenacity to keep moving forward.

Conclusion

As you embark on your trading journey, understand that setbacks and challenges are part of the process. Use this book as a resource to boost your confidence and build a mindset that can withstand the ups and downs of the market. Whether you're starting afresh or picking up from where you left off, remember that the journey is long, but every step you take brings you closer to your goals.

In the next chapter, we'll delve into what to do and what not to do as you start your trading journey. We'll explore practical tips to help you stay on track and build a sustainable path to success.

4.2 Expectations, Mentorship, and All About Starting Out

When people decide to start trading, they often dive in with high expectations, influenced by flashy success stories and social media posts promising quick riches. However, it's crucial to understand that trading is not a get-rich-quick scheme. It's a business that requires time, effort, and a structured approach. This chapter will guide you through managing expectations, the importance of mentorship, and key points to remember as you start your trading journey.

Managing Expectations: The Reality Check

Trading is not like a typical job where you study for years, get a degree, and then find employment with a steady income. In trading, expectations can become your biggest enemy if they are not aligned with reality. Many new traders come in with unrealistic expectations of making huge profits quickly, only to face disappointment when the market doesn't cooperate.

The Illusion of Quick Profits

New traders often think they can open an account, invest some capital, and start making 5x or 10x profits immediately. This is far from the truth. The market is unpredictable and can be brutal. Initial successes can create a false sense of security, leading traders to believe that consistent high returns are easy to achieve. When the inevitable losses come, it hits hard, leading to frustration and demotivation.

The Importance of a Balanced Perspective

To avoid the pitfalls of unrealistic expectations, it's important to approach trading with a balanced perspective. Understand that profits and losses are part of the game. Just like any other business, you will face ups and downs. The key is to manage your risks and keep learning from each experience. Stop expecting the market to always go in your favor. Instead, focus on understanding the market and making informed decisions.

The Role of Mentorship: Finding Your Guide

Behind every successful trader, there's often a mentor who has guided them through the complexities of the market. A mentor is someone who has navigated the turbulent waters of trading and can provide invaluable insights and support. They help you develop the psychological strength, mindset, and skills needed to succeed.

Why You Need a Mentor

A mentor plays a critical role in shaping your trading journey. They provide direction and help you avoid common mistakes. More importantly, they help you see your potential and guide you towards becoming the best version of yourself. With their experience and knowledge, mentors can fill in the gaps in your understanding and help you connect the dots in your trading strategy.

Finding the Right Mentor

To benefit from mentorship, you need to find the right mentor. Look for someone with extensive experience and a proven track record in trading. This person should have navigated various market conditions and cycles, offering a wealth of practical knowledge and insights. A good mentor will analyze your behavior patterns and understand what you lack, helping you grow as a trader.

Embracing Constructive Criticism

Constructive criticism is a vital tool for growth. A good mentor will provide feedback aimed at fostering your development. It's important to differentiate between constructive criticism, which is helpful, and negative criticism, which can be discouraging. Constructive criticism helps you identify areas for improvement and develop better trading habits.

Here are some examples of how constructive criticism from a mentor can help:

1. Risk Management:

- ➢ **Scenario:** You consistently risk a large portion of your capital on a single trade.

- ➢ **Mentor's Advice:** "You're taking too much risk on individual trades. Limit your exposure to no more than 2-3% of your total capital per trade to protect yourself from significant losses."

- ➢ **Action:** Adjust your risk management strategy according to your mentor's advice and monitor the impact on your trading performance.

2. Trade Analysis:

- ➢ **Scenario:** You frequently enter trades based on unreliable information rather than solid analysis.

- ➢ **Mentor's Advice:** "Your entries seem impulsive. Focus on developing a disciplined approach using technical and fundamental analysis. Review your trades to understand why you entered and exited them."

- ➢ **Action:** Spend more time analyzing charts and market data before trading and keep a detailed record of your analysis for future review.

3. Emotional Discipline:

- ➢ **Scenario:** You panic and close trades prematurely or hold onto losing positions too long.

- ➢ **Mentor's Advice:** "Your emotional reactions are affecting your decisions. Implement stop-loss and take-profit orders to automate exits and reduce emotional interference."

- ➤ **Action:** Set predefined stop-loss and take-profit levels for all trades and adhere to them, regardless of market fluctuations.

4. Continuous Improvement:

- ➤ **Scenario:** You rely on outdated strategies that no longer perform well in current market conditions.
- ➤ **Mentor's Advice:** "The market evolves, and so should your strategies. Update your approach to align with current trends and data."
- ➤ **Action:** Research and incorporate new strategies or indicators, backtest them, and adjust your trading plan accordingly.

Starting Out: Key Points to Remember

1. Treat Trading as a Business:

- ➤ Approach trading with the seriousness it deserves. Like any business, it requires planning, strategy, and constant learning.

2. Set Realistic Goals:
- ➢ Start with small, achievable goals. Avoid setting high, unrealistic expectations that can lead to disappointment.

3. Embrace Learning:
- ➢ The market is ever-changing. Commit to continuous learning and stay updated with new trends and strategies.

4. Be Patient:
- ➢ Success in trading doesn't happen overnight. Be prepared for a journey that involves both wins and losses.

5. Find a Mentor:
- ➢ Look for a mentor who can guide you through your trading journey, provide valuable insights, and help you grow.

Conclusion

Starting out in trading can be overwhelming, but with the right mindset and guidance, it can also be incredibly rewarding. Manage your expectations, seek out a mentor, and be open to constructive criticism. Treat trading as a journey of continuous learning and improvement. In the next chapter, we'll delve deeper into the dos and don'ts for new traders, providing practical tips to help you navigate the initial stages of your trading journey with confidence.

4.3 The Ultimate Call

Throughout this book, we've explored the foundations of trading, delved into mindset development, and outlined process-driven strategies to help you embark on your trading journey with confidence. As we reach this chapter, you might feel like it's a conclusion—but it's just the beginning. You've come so far, and it's essential not to let all the time and effort you've invested go to waste. Some of you may be eager to start trading, some might still be hesitant, and others may be excited to continue learning.

The Infinite Learning Journey

In the vast world of trading, the learning never truly ends. The internet is brimming with resources, tutorials, and roadmaps that promise to teach you every aspect of trading. But remember, no matter how much content you consume or how many experts you follow, the ultimate decision and the drive to succeed rest with you. Finding the right mentor or community is invaluable, but never let yourself become overly dependent on anyone.

Self-Reliance and Independence

One crucial lesson to take away from this book is the importance of self-reliance. While it's beneficial to have good mentorship and a supportive community, relying too much on others can be detrimental. Dependence on others not only burdens them but also undermines your own growth. It can make you appear like a "heavy baggage" and nobody wants to carry someone else's load indefinitely.

People may start to underestimate you and show their resentment through actions, leading to lost opportunities and diminished personal growth.

The Roles and Responsibilities of a Trader

As a trader, you wear many hats and shoulder significant responsibilities. You are in charge of your own capital, and losing it can be a daunting nightmare. It's crucial to cultivate your skills continuously and never stop learning. Remember, nobody knows everything. Everyone's journey is unique, shaped by different experiences and paths. Failure is an inevitable part of this journey, and it's something we all face in due time.

A Personal Journey

Think about a young boy, just 15 years old, with a simple ambition: to make money and become rich. He could never have imagined that he would one day master the intricacies of the market, build a thriving community, and teach others the skills he had painstakingly learned. Reflecting on my own journey, I am proud of what I have achieved and am passionate about guiding thousands of others on their paths.

From the very beginning, I was eager to learn, but I knew that patience and discipline were the first principles I needed to internalize. These traits have been the cornerstone of my success and are essential for anyone looking to thrive in trading.

Your Path to Growth

Your choices define your growth. The market favors those who remain calm and composed amid volatility. Developing a solid trading plan is crucial; it's your roadmap to navigating the complexities of the market. This plan should include:

- **Risk Management Strategies:** How much are you willing to risk on each trade? Setting these parameters helps you protect your capital.

- **Entry and Exit Points:** Clearly define when you will enter or exit a trade based on your analysis. This prevents impulsive decisions driven by emotions.

- **Trade Analysis Methods:** Determine the tools and strategies you will use to analyze trades. This could be technical indicators, fundamental analysis, or a combination of both.

Reflection and Moving Forward

As you reflect on everything you've learned and experienced so far, remember this powerful truth: "The biggest obstacle in trading is often the one staring back at you in the mirror." – Alexander Elder. Your mindset, discipline, and commitment to continuous learning are the keys to overcoming this obstacle.

Trading is not just about making money; it's about growing as an individual and becoming resilient in the face of challenges. Keep pushing forward, stay curious, and embrace the journey with an open mind. The path to success in trading is long and filled with ups and downs, but with the right mindset and a solid plan, you can navigate it successfully.

Conclusion

This chapter is not an end but a call to action. Use the knowledge and insights you've gained to start your trading journey or to elevate it to new heights. Stay committed to your growth, remain adaptable, and never stop learning. As you embark on this journey, remember that your success lies in your hands, and with perseverance and dedication, you can achieve your trading goals.

www.ingramcontent.com/pod-product-compliance
Lightning Source LLC
LaVergne TN
LVHW061554070526
838199LV00077B/7048